DISCARD

TROUBLE

Books by Mary Baine Campbell

Poetry:
  The World, the Flesh, and Angels
  Trouble

Scholarly:
  The Witness and the Other World: Exotic European
    Travel Writing, 400–1600
  Wonder and Science: Imagining Worlds in Early
    Modern Europe

Trouble

Poems by
Mary Baine Campbell

Carnegie Mellon University Press
Pittsburgh 2003

Acknowledgments

The following poems have appeared before (some in slightly different versions):

The Black Warrior Review (in a chapbook, "Are Sin, Disease and Death Real?"): "Calm Before the Storm," "Midsummer Night's Dream," "Trouble," "The Cold War," "Eating Poison," "Animals and Infants Cannot Speak," "Sleeping Together: An Encore," "Before the Phone Rang," "Between Moons," "Evening Light 1992," "Back to Nature," "To the Editor," "*Le Monstre Est Vivant*," "The Invisible World" (as "Looking, Older"), "Envoi, or, A Preface to *The Book of the Dead*"; *The Southwest Review*: "The Kiss"; *Field*: "The Michael Jackson Interview"; *The Boston Phoenix*: "The Arrows of Desire"; *The New Yorker*: "Life After Death (II)"; *Ariel*: "The Wound in the Persian Miniature," "Mimesis."

This book would have been impossible without the help of Martha Collins, Robert Hahn, Louisa Solano and, especially, Louise Glück. I am grateful as well for a grant from the Peter S. Reed Foundation, which gave me some precious time. Jason McLachlan is the other author of "A Vision."

The publication of this book is supported by a grant from the Pennsylvania Council on the Arts.

Library of Congress Control Number: 2002101664
ISBN 0-88748-382-8 Pbk.

10 9 8 7 6 5 4 3 2 1

Table of Contents

For Laura Barrows, Daria Donnelly, John Engstrom,
Eve Sedgwick, Jenny Wilson
and
In memoriam, Sheila Ann King, 1957–2000

Thank you.

I

Well

I keep dreaming that all is well.
It takes hours to surface from dreams undertaken to mend the
                                                        world
Its waters, its airs, its places. Wake
Is a good word for the path that disappears
Behind me, and for the long look
Backwards and down to salvations
Invisible by day.

/

Calm Before the Storm

Between the Brattle and the bookstore
A hundred yards of wet brick pavement
Fancy with yellow leaves: I wore
A red jacket, carried a red umbrella
Had a little fever, had a little cough
Was alive, passed a newspaper box
Saw no wars in the headlines
Had no bad news from the doctor
Not yet, was alive, was in love
Had waterproof boots on, it was only
A few yards to the bookstore
On an autumn night, the bookstore
Full of good books and yellow light, I was
Still alive, there was no evidence
Of terminal illness, there were no wars
In the headlines, I have always
Loved the fall the beautiful dead
Bodies of the leaves scattered
On the battlefield of earth and my own
Life persisting.

Novocaine

The music is coming from the engine, seven centuries old,
And the words of it say love has changed everything
For the singer and brought him to life, although he is dead,
And through the windshield a brown finch is visible
Muttering among the leaves. Dust over green, the green of
summer's end.

Inside, the dentist explains to her helper that she always insists
On Novocaine for her patients if she sees the slightest facial
twitch.
"I don't *feel* pain—" says one, "—but *I* do," she replies,
"I don't want to feel your pain or be the one
Who gave it." The helper says, "Why?"

I wish the dentist had answered, but the time had come
To concentrate on my tooth, which was finally numb.
So I lay in the eye of the lamp that brightened the face
Of Dustin Hoffman in *Marathon Man*, in a Hollywood gym
Where the world entered the innocent patient through his
teeth and gums.

The lamp hurt my eyes. I closed them, and thought of the real
pain
Of Mengele's real Jews. But Dr. Bernstein
Was incredibly gentle, in their honor, I guess, in their memory.
She honored my nerves as though they were the nerves of the
world,
Not wanting to feel the pain of the world or be the one who
gave it.

So the stanza the pain should be in is missing here,
Like a book about your disease in the library of what you need.

What good could it be to hear the tale of Novocaine
When "anaesthetic" means artless or missing a sense of the
                                                    beautiful?
But believe me, Dr. Bernstein was artful, and she was also
                                                    beautiful.

The music came in on the P.A., seven centuries old,
And the troubadour's words say love has changed everything
For him and brought him to life, though of course he's dead.
The sun is higher and summer's an hour older and Dr.
                                            Bernstein too
Is singing for no reason as she takes off her surgical mask.

The Wound in the Persian Miniature

The wound was a detail
Drawn with a single-hair brush.
It didn't hurt, it was like
Caressing a fly with your
Corner eyelash. I mean
It didn't hurt the painter.
And of course it didn't hurt
The paint. The wound
Was a gash in heaven.
At night the sun slices
The skin at the horizon line
And slips through on a slur
Of bloody cloud. The sky aches
And a few dewy stars
Spill from its eye. The lashes
Are comets: they say
There will be more wounds
For everyone. For the child
On the glittering beach
Where the Heinekens lie in shards,
For the child on the front
Page, and for everyone
She knew. The last wound
Comes at last. A surgical slit
In the case, the world. And you
Leak through.

Our Childhood

At the Taft Hotel in New York, 1963
We were really happy—allowed to watch
The Lucy Show between the bars of light:
Beloved Venetian blinds which are only seen
In the outside world, which we also terribly loved.

That room was all one color: liver
Was the 60s name for the rug, the walls
The bricks of the air shaft, the soot
That shrouded the TV's greenish screen—
I guess that's two colors.

And Lucy, the bluish-gray of video
Was another color still. As was my dress,
Organdy, with big pink roses printed
On every diaphanous layer of grayish-white.
Neither my sapphire eyes nor my brother's

Emeralds count though. They were not
In the picture, it was in them. The picture
Of the outside world that had supplied
And washed the muslin curtains, and built
A tower sixteen stories high to hold us up.

The picture of a large gray strawberry blonde
With charcoal mouth screaming and a throat like the airshaft's
                                                    shadow
In which she stored the scream her adventure
Always led her to. We felt that *our* adventure
Would end well, without shock or fear.

Later the Taft Hotel was in the movies—brown and gold
And scarlet. Mrs. Robinson met Dustin Hoffman there for love
one night.
But that was after all New York had disappeared
In black and white, in a flurry of pigeon wings: *Failsafe*:
We saw it on TV in 1968.

TROUBLE

1. The Kiss

The kiss turned into a different kiss,
The man turned into another man.
He left. It was cold on the hillside
In the dark. I read the diary
Of the woman he really loved.

All kisses come to this at last.
When I woke up my friends began to call.
One had kissed a man who stole
Her violin, the other a man
She had left like a terrible vice.

Their voices were druggy and slow
With desires resisted. I told them both
To go and get kissed again.
Not that the world is about to end
Or age come calling soon,

But all kisses are fate, and all fate
In the end is an end. Why fight?
That warm mouth may lie to you
Later. Now it is speechless
With the tongue of an angel.

2. *Midsummer Night's Dream*

Two days before the war of all
Against all I began to pack
A minimum of small, compressible goods.
I moved rarely and carefully:
The greed had begun, and anyone
Might steal from me. I thought
Of what I needed all the time.
Paper: I would have to learn
To write small. The calendar
On the wall, but it would run out
In six months. Still, it would provide
A chronological bridge. I made
One trip to the store, for cigarettes.
If I smoke one or two a day
The carton will last as long
As the calendar. I will need
Those little sedatives. I could not
Go cold turkey in the middle
Of total war. I forget what else
I packed. Only what I needed
Out of all this, only what I had
To have. No land, no money. You
Were halfway across the end
Of the world; did I pack
A photograph? What did I do?

3. *Trouble*

You haven't told me what to do
So I can't. Did I fall asleep
For a moment, watching the burro
Cross the back yard, into the trees?
Did I go with the burro
Into the dark and lose your voice—
Did you say something after all?
Probably so. I often forgot you.
You brought us to live in a place
So beautiful we lost our minds.
(On the burro's back I went far
Far away. The trees pressed close
Together, scheming, littering
In a moonless dark.
Just as despair began, I saw
A light in the distance, winking
At the forester's door.
An owl tried to tear out my hair, a wolf
Scuffled in the litter. It's hard
To reach safety, or even to be on the way.)

To Autumn

These autumn days in Winchester were the last of
happy health for Keats.
      —H. E. S., ed., Cambridge edition of
            The Complete Poetical Works

I

Another poet might be ecstatic by now
This orange afternoon in October: the thick paint
On the roof trim glares neon in the day's late light;
I've just seen a blue jay chasing an actual bee
Out of the eaves and into the yellowing oak
And something is definitely twittering, it's not
My imagination. I sit here,
As the saying goes, by the window—
Looking for the dirty bits in
The Best American Poetry, 1994
I am indolent, in a writerly way,
Having been up late last night, trying
To understand *The Golden Book of Astronomy,*
The millions of miles it illustrates,
The compensating optics it explains.
No book is completely satisfying. I get hung
Up on the way a lens will turn things upside
Down. I get lost. I dreamed a little girl
Monkey was hanging upside down
From a nest in the eaves. She dropped
Out of sight, into empty space;
She is faraway now, or I am
And the poets write about desire:
I remember specific
Body parts and what they do
When they are touched.

II

There is no one there on the granary floor.
There is no one watching by the cider press.
How could I be ecstatic when Fall
Has fallen from the eaves into
An indescribable space?

Sometimes a window is just a window.
As always, I want something more.
Like the fist that shatters it
Over and over
In *Terminator*
And *Terminator II*. A mist *has* come
Tonight, in fact, and in it thousands
Of ghosts, if ghosts are made
Of the water and dust into which my friends,
The dead, divide. What lifts our hair is,
As the poet says, a "*winnowing* wind."

Hearing

I

The old men and the kings
Are rioting—their teeth gnash
So loud we can hear it
On TV and in our sleep,
Fat guys in suits
Light fuses, roar, push buttons,
Tear the houses down
And scare us with their claws
And fangs and wings
And wake us up. No one
Can stop them, night
And day, their cries
Clutter the air waves
Pierce the windows
Bomb the pillows
Topple trees, punch holes
In sky, from every
  mountainside
    etc.

II

Although it is very late
And no moon, she stepped
Through a hole in the wall
And found food—Pampers
And light bulbs too. Her friend
Went to the shoe store:

"This is the first time
All six of my children
Have had shoes that fit."

III

It is very late
And no moon.
If the shoe fits
Wear it.
If the bough breaks
Hush.

IV

Every move is a message
Every sound is a message
Your face could be
A message, your dead
Body, your children
When they are not
Too scared to cry. You
Are a message: you say
Please bleeding mute unconscious
Please people weeping please
Face down on the ground please
54, 55, 56 motionless please
We can get along.

Above It All

If you see fire below
It must be a whole city.
It looks like a candle. Maybe
It's New Year's Eve. It's pretty.

The countryside is Mondrian.
Some Jackson Pollack splatter
Means wilderness, here and there.
By night it's a map of the stars.

In first class the drinks are free
And the babies don't cry.
In coach, somebody passes
The stewardess a note.

There's an ill wind pouring in
From the fuselage. Low-income
Fanatics have a gun
Pointed at your head.

Suddenly everything looks real—
More like Vermeer. You can see
Yourself reflected in the window
And the fear on your face.

It isn't safe up here, so high
Above the earth. Up here
Is for angels. Human, even
The terrorists are afraid.

Furs

I am Cruella, getting out of a cab,
My coat made of puppy skins
Slips off one shoulder and snow
Touches my own skin there: smoke
Enters me through an ivory stem.

Men fear me and scurry: I must
Be an astrological sign. The street
Is slippery, but who would dare
To let me fall? One twelfth
Of the universe is under my spell.

When the show is over we'll ride
My Rolls in the blizzard—out
To the innocent farms, careening
In snowlight among hedgerows
Hunting: perhaps I am the goddess of that.

Like all beautiful women I'm wicked
And frigid: the only men around
Are Disney henchmen. I am interested
In the pain of animals and children,
I want to get inside their skins.

In a thousand dark places, children
Watch my moving image, wanting
Something. They love the little dogs
But can't help wondering: will her coat
Be hung with four hundred paws?

I am not afraid to kill: beauty
Is the most important matter.
I share with the children their love
For the dogs, and they share with me
My feeling for fashion, and moonlight, and snow.

The Cold War

It was dark all the way from our chairs
To the end of space.
There were no stars—*no stars*,
Do you know what that means?
I could see you, though,
And the gray concrete of the terrace
At our feet, and the edge
Of the emerald lawn, elegant
Against the dead black matte
Of the burgled sky: for a moment
I could see you as the bomb
Burst in our eyes. We died
And rose again with whiplash
In the dark and the bomb
Burst in our eyes. We died
And rose again with whiplash
In the dark. The bomb
Was merciless that year—
It fell and fell, like rain,
Like angry blows, but it çame
From nowhere and meant nothing.

Eating Poison

Dogs know to eat grass when they're sick:
It smells like the right thing to do.
They get better, they come back
Into the world, they play. Why,
If babies are animals, did I consume
Cigarettes, rat poison? If dogs
Are hardwired to self-medicate surely
A human baby's genes don't require
Suicide? Why did I keep on
Eating those things? Day after day.

*

In the refulgence of midafternoon
I could see well enough, even in the dark medicine
Closet, to climb towards certain objects.

*

I learned to roll off beds and counters early.
Knocked my head up and later it gave birth
To a darkness that won't lift. But I can
See in the dark. I can read
Labels that say no. Don't. Decorated
With the pirates' flag, Roger, the jolly skull
Lip-syncing "Live free or die."

Nightfall

The sun is going down here
Bringing on thoughts of mercy
While on the opposite world
She is rising, full of fire and ambition.

Her feet touch the cold floor
And she flinches in spite of herself.
It is not always easy, I suppose,
To do what she does—

To topple those other powers
And reestablish her reign
Every day, to spare none,
To lose nothing.

Wherever I can spot
A flicker in the strong light
Of conquest I can rest
My tired eyes. I love

The dark coming on, enclosing
My world in mercy. Battles
Stop for the night and it is time
To eat and read. In sleep

We are all available as deer
To Death, which nearly always
Spares us. We can learn
From Sleep and Death to risk

Our openness, and to relent. So
As her spears fly out
In the opposite world, I catch her
Round the ankles like a cat

Or a warrior vanquished: Please
Stop shining. Come to my world
Where you are fading into mercy,
Going down. Learn to relent, like Death.

The First Week of Spring

Sooner or later, the work is done:
The firmament divided,
A world shaped, great whales
Swimming and singing in the deep—
Your very own deep,
Beyond whose beaches wave
In a homemade wind
Your final subtlety, the grasses.
You know it's good
But there is no one there
To say so. Wind and grass
Whisper and touch, the whales
Dive and the firmaments
Mingle in a storm.
Your idle hands are shaping mud pies
After the rain. You sigh.
You look closer. "Mud," you say,
As if this were not a man,
Too happy yet to answer you.

Life After Death (II)

The pharaoh was buried with a hundred
Little stone doppelgängers instead
Of his servants.

They were all different sizes but compared to the pharaoh
They were all small. Each had his own
Face. There were no stone wives or lovers.

Not one could lift his hand to help.
To face the length of death the pharaoh
Had gathered around him men
Of enduring stuff.

They stood at attention, or lay
In the rubble of the grave, stiff
With love, or is it rigid with fear?

You can't tell, and you can't ask. But you can guess
How joy flexed the models' muscles
Later, on their way to the baths.

Animals and Infants Cannot Speak

Seen from above the hurricane
Is a belly of cloud. Its empty navel
Winds earthwards like a cord
To the infant house, sleeping
In the storm's dark eye.

Alone in the corner room, I'm hungry
Eating wind. A squirrel in the tree
Starves with me, speechless, full
Of the same unsatisfying rage.

It rustles the leaves. Like a windstorm—
Except where we are is peace.

Full Moon

The moon goes aching up into the sky
Like a hand searching
For peaches on the highest shelf.

I am watching so slowly I can see
The whole bright arm
Lifted from the shoulder of moonrise.

The cupboard is empty. The hungry moon
Discovers every night
There is nothing up there but itself.

II

LONG DISTANCE

1. Direct Address

These poems are a voice composed
At home alone to answer
Yours—a voice so rich
Even the telephone turns
To gold at your call.

I never stop answering.
You never stop calling.
The gold piles up like sunlight
On a lake. We cannot spend it
Or speak of it.

At noon, water-gold and sun-gold
Mingle: the lake exhales
Into the sky. The sky inhales
The lake. No one has broken
The real silence of love.

2. Sleeping Together: An Encore

for JSM

At midnight, things appear
In their true sizes. Because
The moon is full
I know you are lying above me
With one eye shut
To focus better. The rest
Of your body is dark
As this benighted continent
But warmer, resting on me
Breathing trustfully. I know
How to care for your vast
Body and how to protect
The deer beneath your branches
And your thoughts, the owls.

When day comes we forget
How deeply we rested,
How close we were together.
It seems as if we are far away
And small, earning money
And operating machines, but
After the sun goes down
We are giants again, Atlantic
And Pacific lapping
One long shore.

3. Before the Phone Rang

If I could talk to you. With my mouth.
It must be a real mouth. Some words
Are in it like my tongue. Flesh
And blood are just two of them.

I can't talk to you but if I could.
And listen back. My ear quaking,
Its tiny machine quaking with sound,
Your voice in my cilia, loud light waving

So many thousand miles. Flesh
And blood both places. Oblivious
Mountains in between and animals
Minding invisible business.

If I could talk. If you would listen.
The air would be full of us
Meeting like this. Invisible business
Made flesh, and less oblivion.

4. Between Moons

Poetry no longer beautiful
And you gone, gone
And even the moon
The third thing I love
Keeps vanishing.

"Vanish" is wrong—
What we love darkens
With time or pain darkens it
But it is not
Ever gone.

It is hidden in us
Like a great grief in a woman
Of self-control or a planet
In a planet's shadow
Or the meanings of words.

Mimesis

The living woman is carving a dead one from stone.
She pauses, depressed, resting her chisel
Where the breastbone will be, if
She does not pause too long, if
She can bear to strike.

Their gazes do not meet: the imaginary
Woman has closed her dead stone eyes.
Of course the sculptor could force them open
With her instrument. But then what?

The woman of stone has other business.
Inside the sculpted lines the life
Of minerals persists. Crystal and grit
Remember the laws of their kind
And lastingly obey.

The living woman is violent. Her quarrel
Has been handled with weapons so far
But the stone woman will not die.
She is more and more her immemorial
Self with every blow.

The living woman must finish this.
She was hired to complete an effigy
And she needs the pay. In the air
Of evening, outside the studio, the sparrows
Chatter about their food. Then flicker away.

The Singer

Men who wish to sing dress up like women—
In the dresses of the past, or of the East.
Even Tom Jones with his plunging neckline
And tight black pants looks like Edie Gormé.
It is the only way they can permit you
To stare at their trembling throats:
A woman is someone with a trembling throat.

Women who wish to speak dress up like singers.
They tune the vibrators in their throats
And cover themselves in ancient silk.
Lights flare before and behind them, red lips
Open to show the white gates of the teeth
Which open to show the tongue, native
Or of angels, not kissing you now
But singing the words of their manifestos.

Drenched in the sight of the singer it's hard
To take notes on notes, and you wore your own
Best dress to be here, being her, not meaning
What she means but receiving the love
You give her from your seat in the balcony
Above her. It's all so beautiful, and so are you
With your pupils wide open like doorways
And the singer inside them, beckoning.

Like anyone that slinky, the singer's being
Paid, but there's more pain in her voice
Than you bought or could use. Although

The occasion for so much silk,
She sounds in some phrases like real birds
Hungry and small out there, and wondering
Whether they'll live.

II

A bird who wishes to sing is starving, or warning
Or getting directions: Here
I am, here I am, she sings, In this tree.
Where are you? Trembling he sings, Here I am
Are you there? Here I am. I'm hungry
Where are you, I'm here, Is there anything there?
There's a cat. Here I am. Where are you.

—And in the bedrooms of the world, we shudder awake
As if to music, as if to a kind of song.

Evening Light 1992

Chaucer lived above a city gate,
The one the revolting peasants entered by,
The murmurynge churles—the iron
At your throat, the life
And not the art. And so do I.

And so do you. The TV's on,
The cars outside are rushing to their dooms,
One of the children playing
In the street will grow to be
A murderer, and murder you.

Or murder me, and rightly so.
This nest's rare feathers float on blood.
In golden evening, how to count
The cost of shimmering, the lines
The feet, the rhymes, the perished dead?

Back to Nature

In memoriam Angela Carter (1940–1992)

Very few women are born
In the hospital. Most of them
Are reared by wolves. This is why
They find it so hard
To wear shoes, or play
The harpsichord, or speak.

If you let a woman out
Of your sight for an instant
She'll revert. Peeling down
To her pelt and paws, she'll leap
At the moon through any window.
How to explain that crash of figurines
The neighbors surely heard?

She is not absolutely safe
Even in the choir:
Beware the soprano voice,
The animal descant,
The code that cracks glass.
Outside the church
A sharp-toothed congregation
Listens in its own way.

To the Editor

Dear Sir:

First your columnist says it's sacred.
Then he says there's nothing a flagburner can't "say"
Just the same by writing it on a poster
Or just saying it. How can that be
If the flag is sacred?
Why doesn't he just run a poster up the flagpole
And wait to see who salutes?
Is his little paean to the flag the same thing
As a flag? If it is, I want him to know
I burnt it.

Thank God there's no constitutional amendment
Against burning words. I'm going to burn
The Constitution. I'm going to burn
The Declaration of Independence.
Every morning before I go to work
I'm going to write THE FLAG
On a piece of paper and use it to light
The dawn's early cigarette.
I'm going to burn "The Star-Spangled Banner"—
I'm even going to burn the melody.

But it won't be enough,
Because words aren't sacred and tunes aren't either
And neither were the twenty postage stamps
With flags on them I burnt yesterday
Along with a dollar bill for good luck.

I haven't put my torch to a temple yet
Because your columnist says The Flag
Is the only sacred thing in America.

Burning a temple's just arson: I want
To desecrate something, really desecrate it
Top to bottom, inside and out
I want to desecrate it till it's white hot
Till it begs me to stop, till it flags, till it folds up
Like a flower when the nuclear sun goes down
At last and in the peace of the night
Real lovers turn to each other, flame
To shining flame.

The Michael Jackson Interview

"Nature takes its course."
—Michael Jackson, to Oprah Winfrey

Michael Jackson is walking across the lawn,
Is walking across the universe.
That constellation is The Ferris Wheel
And all those bald-headed children
Have cancer. They are going to fly
Among the stars for a few minutes.
They are going to take his prayers to heaven.

Michael Jackson has a skin disease.
He is turning into a white
Woman who looks a lot
Like his best friend Brooke Shields.
When they kiss they cannot
Tell each other apart.

Michael Jackson might live forever.
He has the background for it
And the personality.
Standing behind Elizabeth Taylor
He showed a King Tut profile.
When the smoke alarm went off
He didn't blink.

Age cannot wither him, nor custom stale
His infinite variety. A ghost, a clown,
A china doll, a girl, stormtrooper, Jesus,
Werewolf, Diana Ross, the World,
Mother Theresa, Pharaoh, motherless child,
Michael Valentine Smith
Or Michelangelo, a child

Whose father beat him, who died to sin,
Whose father beat him again
And again. Beat him again
And again and again. Beat him again.
Beat him again. Beat him.

Kidnapped

You can never come all the way back
From the Land of the Dead—
The dead are jealous friends
And they fed you their food,
You slept in their cots.
For the rest of your life
You will remember their names
And the words for things
We never speak of here.
For the rest of your life
The living will seem sweet
But infantile: the dead alone
Have seen the world.

You will enjoy America, the cartoons
And picnic tables of your kin.
But always beneath the soil
The ninepins rolling, the crude jokes
Of the underworld. You'll go down
At last, like the rest of us,
But for you it will be different.
You know where they live
And exactly how to get there.

Le Monstre Est Vivant

The terrible baby is 9/10 out of me
Feet first, if those are feet,
And willing as a stone.
It's taking years. No name
Will stick to such a thing, I fear.

I'm sorry, I can't help you right now
I'm having a monster.
Would you get the police?
Can you give me something?
For it?

What if it gets loose?
Hasn't got a face?
But I must be calm
And love it. In fact
It could be of some use—
Its miraculous birth
And my extreme terror.
I don't mean I could make money off it
In the yellow press. I mean
If it stayed close
And I could stand it, it would tell me
What to say: I could say
Almost anything
About a thing like that.

Snapshot World

Everyone is shy and awkward
And having a good time
And everyone is still alive.

Everyone is touching
And laughing for posterity.
Faces perform nothing but love.

It is always crowded. The room
Is lightning-blue and the laughing eyes
Glare like the eyes of shocked wolves.

Outside—but there is no outside.
And no one sulks in the corner
Refusing to be photographed;

No one is left out or weeping
Or wondering what to say next.
No one has fled to the roof

To howl at the moon. What moon?
That flaming nimbus at the window
Is a craze in the lens.

Crematorium

So tender was the fire it blossomed
In lilies of flame, in forget-me-nots
Of flame: among the petals men
Already dead lay dappled like Ophelia
In her little river, under the spring leaves.
Afterlives snatched at them the way
A ring of girls in a pastoral will snatch
At columbines, magnolia, flame azalea
Falling back to earth over their heads
In a luxury of windblown flowers, falling,
Wherever they're not caught into the mud
At the river's edge, into the lists
Of the actuary, into death notices, back pages,
Into the dark hands of the auctioneer
And the mud that packs his goods
Away at last.

A Vision

The city was falling and the night around it was mean,
The stars were falling and the night was nervous and mean.
The living people looked down at their feet, or across
At each other with knives in their nervous eyes—
They did their usual crimes and they drove their cars
Like they didn't care if a lot of people died.

The man in the room at night was hard at work
On something electrically powered, he needed a few
More feet of extension cord. Stars falling and all,
He didn't know where at such an hour to go
And the night outside at the end of an era was scared—
The stars were falling and the night they fell in was mean.

Two strangers across town planned to sell everything
On Saturday morning and move to the ends of the earth
And they'd hung up a sign, Ambrose and Virginia. The man
Called up on the phone and drove to their house in the dead
Of night, to the city's other side, across the dark,
His eyes wide open and all his windows closed.

Ambrose and Virginia had wire, the man wire twists
Like you use to close bags at the top, and they wanted those.
So the deal was done, and a smile was smiled all around,
For these were the three Just Ones, and to prove it was so
The man as he left saw a tiny stick on the ground
At the end of which a tiny toucan and a cat
Were sitting in friendship, as quiet as they were small.

A vision like that is not a promise of peace:
It might have been the last one, in the world we know.
But as needs were met and the night survived by three,
A cat and a toucan sat on the end of a stick.

The Dreadful Has Already Happened

Last week, roped together, three men fell
Two thousand feet on Mt. Rainier, from ice
To ice in the summer air.

It was roughly the anniversary
Of Nagasaki, the one we forget,
The after-math, the also-dropped.

And many have died on that day
Since that day, and many died hard,
But such a long fall, and for nothing:

As if the world and its brilliant physics
Had no more heart than a bomb
Which implodes on its emptiness.

The men who fell had time to see
The antlers of the deer wheel by
And the earth rise up from another place.

Many more will fall. Many bombs
Will fall, and cities will fall, and terror
Fall on us, and with us, and the sky come down.

It will be the worse for us because
We have fallen already, we have already
Been dropped.

Making Believe

It is like nothing in nature. This rage
Hamstrung one leg, or lit the nerve on fire,
Broke both feet and tore my biggest teeth
In half. I'm sure you yourself wake up
At dawn or before with aching jaws
And one shoulder knotted and a ridge
In your forehead like a gutter. The body
Wants to break itself and rend itself.
Or doesn't want to, but has to,
To protect someone else.

If nature were at work here, I could take
This heart, hard and hundreds of red degrees,
And sink it in a distant snow. I might have to go
A long way but if nature were the ground
My feet would not have broken: I could
Walk, and my wrists could bear
The weight of the heart in my hands.
In nature every grown animal is strong enough for her life.

Someone might say, even you, this rage is my nature.
It is not. My nature is, like yours, a stream—
Transparent convolutions, almost bodiless, wash stones
In the bed of this stream where I am lying
And flowing, full of cool wonder,
And fish come through me with such pleasure.
I am nothing like the body that pulls its bones apart
In sleep or at the desk and cannot be calmed
Because it requires murder: the impossible.

Love Song

I

Is she hiding? She is not
Looking like herself, or sounding—
Unless that great gong filling
The air is the sounding
Of her bell.

Unless that black bird whose wing
The wind has bent, still flying
In the highway snow, in the air
Of the bell, is her tracking me,
Pointing me out.

Unless the highway is her lap.
Unless my car is her heart,
Racing for a home beyond
This white horizon. Unless
I am her identical daughter.

II

Why would she deck herself out
Disguised as the world?
It is not her style: too grand.
I would recognize her more easily
With a drink and a cigarette

Or curled in a blanket reading
Almost anything or weeping
And storming in a childhood
She didn't mean to wreck—ah!
Queen of a house, a man, a world?

I would recognize her (helped
By professionals) in dreams
Where she is huge and mad and if
She sees us we will die
Or worse, but here we are.

III

One more time: doesn't everyone
Get one more time after the end?
She is coming towards me across a plain
Lit by fire and I am moving towards her
In the same light; we are twins

At last and getting close: even the red light
Of the endtime shows me how like herself
She looks, if indeed that is her
And not some other, an other coming through a field
Of poppies at high noon, like a sun

Drunk, inhaling flowers, rushing
To me, desire vermilion
In his cheeks and I have stopped
In the middle afraid of the stranger and gazing
Around me at a world. At last.

On Hearing a Distant Sound

Inside the ear's shell
a ring of feeling
at the tunnel's rim startles
and fills itself
from the bronze ripples
of the bell.

Like a deer drinking in last
light startles, sees nothing
and drinks,
after the violence
of the bell, imagining
all is well.

In the ear's darkness
the sound wells, like the deer's
pool—it floods, it gathers
force, ends, like the ear's nerves
in the throat, which fills
and cannot tell.

Charm

Let this day come:
Let it stir in its dark shawl
And let the birds speak of it
Sleepily at first and then
Let them be astonished
And celebrate loudly
Her iridescent skin
Where it shows at the edge
Of the soft shawl:
At the neck of morning
At her wrists, which the birds
Announce, amazed.

Let this day come closer
Dropping her shawl,
Let her lie down
On the damp ground
Naked and roped in pearls
And let her cause a commotion
Among the scampering
Animals, and let her wake
Even the city, even the cathouse
With the brightness of her eye.

Let the televisions go on
In her honor, bright-eyed
Like day and chattering
Like her winged announcers.
Let the jackhammer pound
The street in desire
And the trucks dash
Thundering everywhere, burdened
With food and searching
For her altar to unload.

The Invisible World

Getting older, the flesh around my head
And neck gets looser, like a hood.
I move around inside invisible
But for the bright turtle-eye, the part that sees.

When I was five I rode a turtle at the zoo.
I've seen the picture, and remember it.
The four right angles represent
My father's single giant eye.

The turtle they said was here before Columbus was—
Not in the zoo but in the world.
His eye from the right angle looks half dark,
Empty, but lit as if by milk.

Can he see at all? It's hard to tell
Because the world beyond my father's giant eye,
The world he would be looking at
Is gone. I move around invisible, inside.

The Arrows of Desire

The bronzed body of St. Sebastian
Leaned out at me from a poster
At the Art Institute, bristling
With ivory-feathered arrows.

He did not bleed because
He had no time for anything
But desire. His muscles
Strained to reach me.

Even before I arrived
He was leaning out of the frame—
Or into the sharp sensation
Of the arrowheads.

They are coming from behind us,
From out of this world.
To reach his gleaming, penetrable skin
They pass through me

Over and over, carrying something
Into his heart and his arms
Which is not Christian,
Though a god is involved.

Empyrean

Endlessly not heaven the sky
Goes on and on and the problem
With human life is that
Although there is nothing
Behind the blue but more
Blue we can't see as far
As it goes. Or if we had a ship
We can't go there, although
It's the same as here
So who cares?

Or if we had a rocket we can't
Go there. Or if we had a rocket
And a thousand years.
Or if we could ride a light ray
And had a thousand
Thousand years and our cells
Never broke down and our hearts
Never broke down and our eyes
Stayed fixed on the far blue,
Which isn't blue, and didn't dim

For a thousand thousand years—
Still we could never go there
And even if we could land
On that final blue beach,
Then what? Your cells would burst
At last, your heart break
Remembering me gone mortal
So long ago and so far away,
As mine breaks now, bearing this
Immensity of blue.

The Wake

The child is holding the hand
Of another child he does not care for
But cares for now, now that the taker
Of care is in the ground,
Like the mother of the child
Who is caring for the child he
May not love.
            The dead
Are not only dead to us
But to each other. Where they go
Is very dark, not even a place.
No one is ever there to talk to
Or hold on to. We the living
Are lucky—the child holds on
To the child and I hold on
To them as though they were their mothers
Or my own, who also went
Where she could not be touched
Or spoken to.
            You'd think
The living would hold on
More tightly to each other
But they've learned
A light touch, death
Is everywhere now, teaching
That touch, showing you
How not to leave tracks
In the endless snow.

Death is everywhere now. The living
Stand in circles within circles, teaching
Each other the light touch, touching
Each other lightly—"Time to go."

Death is everywhere now. It's like a flame
That touches every head, even
The heads of those who can't imagine it,
Or couldn't. Now they can.

In medias res

The whirr of the computer booting up,
The high whine of the engine
Furious to leave the earth,
The panic at the start of love—
The soprano tantrums with which
Everything apparently begins—

They cease, they dip. At cruising altitude
There is no fury in the engine
And the sky's as blue, as blank
As three o'clock in the afternoon.

Some people can't stand it. I've read
Three stories in the Globe this month
On people lighting cigarettes in airplanes
In spite of all the tonnage of the law—
Anything to jumble up the level glide
The steadiness, the hum.

But I can stand it. Middle-earth
Is where we live, and in
The middle of things, if not
The center. Here in the midst
Of megadeath I am alive
Eating or flying, loving you

More than I ever did before
And smelling everything as if
For the first time: the hot plastic
Of modern machines, the smoke
In the bathroom—menthol, forbidden,
And the crushed leaves ground into
Your shoes and your beloved skin.

Envoi, or,
A Preface to The Book of the Dead

Here are 189 spells
To be spoken after death
For various purposes.
They are written down
In case you forget them.

With these spells you can make food
And drink appear, prevent
Humiliations to your corpse,
Keep out of trouble with the gods,
Make the grave open
And go abroad by day.
There are spells for becoming a crocodile,
For seeing your old house,
For not dying again.

It may be possible to die
So deeply that you cannot read.
In that case, I admit, this book
Will lie unused in the dirt
By your vanishing
Right hand.

Sonnet à Clef

You like a voice crying in the wilderness
Because you like to be the only one
Who hears, and because you like to hear
A language not only human.

I do long, as I have said before, to be a wolf
Or an owl. Something with a long cry
Never forgotten, never reduced. Not the silvery note
Of a planet though. Something sad.

Anything crying in the wilderness, I guess—
At that distance, it has to be sad.
Out in the wilderness, whatever cries is alone, is lost,
Has forgotten all the words.

(In the valley, in the suburb, in the tree
By the window others, too, have forgotten.)

The Gift of the Magi

What makes it feel impossible
To write a poem or remember
A dream or even to connect
One thing with some other?
What white monster crouches
Having devoured the empty sky?
What word is not spoken
Or whispered or written or cried?
What word, what word
Held back in my throat or yours
And then what answering word
Strangled in yours or mine?
What accusation, what declaration
Of love makes so much silence inside?

CARNEGIE MELLON POETRY SERIES

1975
The Living and the Dead, Ann Hayes
In the Face of Descent, T. Alan Broughton

1976
The Week the Dirigible Came, Jay Meek
Full of Lust and Good Usage, Stephen Dunn

1977
How I Escaped from the Labyrinth and Other Poems, Philip Dacey
The Lady from the Dark Green Hills, Jim Hall
For Luck: Poems 1962-1977, H.L. Van Brunt
By the Wreckmaster's Cottage, Paula Rankin

1978
New & Selected Poems, James Bertolino
The Sun Fetcher, Michael Dennis Browne
A Circus of Needs, Stephen Dunn
The Crowd Inside, Elizabeth Libbey

1979
Paying Back the Sea, Philip Dow
Swimmer in the Rain, Robert Wallace
Far from Home, T. Alan Broughton
The Room Where Summer Ends, Peter Cooley
No Ordinary World, Mekeel McBride

1980
And the Man Who Was Traveling Never Got Home, H.L. Van Brunt
Drawing on the Walls, Jay Meek
The Yellow House on the Corner, Rita Dove
The 8-Step Grapevine, Dara Wier
The Mating Reflex, Jim Hall

1981
A Little Faith, John Skoyles
Augers, Paula Rankin

Walking Home from the Icehouse, Vern Rutsala
Work and Love, Stephen Dunn
The Rote Walker, Mark Jarman
Morocco Journal, Richard Harteis
Songs of a Returning Soul, Elizabeth Libbey

1982
The Granary, Kim R. Stafford
Calling the Dead, C.G. Hanzlicek
Dreams Before Sleep, T. Alan Broughton
Sorting It Out, Anne S. Perlman
Love Is Not a Consolation; It Is a Light, Primus St. John

1983
The Going Under of the Evening Land, Mekeel McBride
Museum, Rita Dove
Air and Salt, Eve Shelnutt
Nightseasons, Peter Cooley

1984
Falling from Stardom, Jonathan Holden
Miracle Mile, Ed Ochester
Girlfriends and Wives, Robert Wallace
Earthly Purposes, Jay Meek
Not Dancing, Stephen Dunn
The Man in the Middle, Gregory Djanikian
A Heart Out of This World, David James
All You Have in Common, Dara Wier

1985
Smoke from the Fires, Michael Dennis Browne
Full of Lust and Good Usage, Stephen Dunn (2nd edition)
Far and Away, Mark Jarman
Anniversary of the Air, Michael Waters
To the House Ghost, Paula Rankin
Midwinter Transport, Anne Bromley

1986
Seals in the Inner Harbor, Brendan Galvin
Thomas and Beulah, Rita Dove

Tall Stranger, Gillian Conoley
The Gathering of My Name, Cornelius Eady
A Dog in the Lifeboat, Joyce Peseroff
Raised Underground, Renate Wood
Divorce: A Romance, Paula Rankin

1992
Modern Ocean, James Harms
The Astonished Hours, Peter Cooley
You Won't Remember This, Michael Dennis Browne
Twenty Colors, Elizabeth Kirschner
First A Long Hesitation, Eve Shelnutt
Bountiful, Michael Waters
Blue for the Plough, Dara Wier
All That Heat in a Cold Sky, Elizabeth Libbey

1993
Trumpeter, Jeannine Savard
Cuba, Ricardo Pau-Llosa
The Night World and the Word Night, Franz Wright
The Book of Complaints, Richard Katrovas

1994
If Winter Come: Collected Poems, 1967–1992, Alvin Aubert
Of Desire and Disorder, Wayne Dodd
Ungodliness, Leslie Adrienne Miller
Rain, Henry Carlile
Windows, Jay Meek
A Handful of Bees, Dzvinia Orlowsky

1995
Germany, Caroline Finkelstein
Housekeeping in a Dream, Laura Kasischke
About Distance, Gregory Djanikian
Wind of the White Dresses, Mekeel McBride
Above the Tree Line, Kathy Mangan
In the Country of Elegies, T. Alan Broughton
Scenes from the Light Years, Anne C. Bromley
Quartet, Angela Ball
Rorschach Test, Franz Wright

1996
Back Roads, Patricia Henley
Dyer's Thistle, Peter Balakian
Beckon, Gillian Conoley
The Parable of Fire, James Reiss
Cold Pluto, Mary Ruefle
Orders of Affection, Arthur Smith
Colander, Michael McFee

1997
Growing Darkness, Growing Light, Jean Valentine
Selected Poems, 1965-1995, Michael Dennis Browne
Your Rightful Childhood: New and Selected Poems, Paula Rankin
Headlands: New and Selected Poems, Jay Meek
Soul Train, Allison Joseph
The Autobiography of a Jukebox, Cornelius Eady
The Patience of the Cloud Photographer, Elizabeth Holmes
Madly in Love, Aliki Barnstone
An Octave Above Thunder: New and Selected Poems, Carol Muske

1998
Yesterday Had a Man In It, Leslie Adrienne Miller
Definition of the Soul, John Skoyles
Dithyrambs, Richard Katrovas
Postal Routes, Elizabeth Kirschner
The Blue Salvages, Wayne Dodd
The Joy Addict, James Harms
Clemency and Other Poems, Colette Inez
Scattering the Ashes, Jeff Friedman
Sacred Conversations, Peter Cooley
Life Among the Trolls, Maura Stanton

1999
Justice, Caroline Finkelstein
Edge of House, Dzvinia Orlowsky
A Thousand Friends of Rain: New and Selected Poems, 1976-1998,
        Kim Stafford
The Devil's Child, Fleda Brown Jackson
World as Dictionary, Jesse Lee Kercheval
Vereda Tropical, Ricardo Pau-Llosa

The Museum of the Revolution, Angela Ball
Our Master Plan, Dara Wier

2000
Small Boat with Oars of Different Size, Thom Ward
Post Meridian, Mary Ruefle
Hierarchies of Rue, Roger Sauls
Constant Longing, Dennis Sampson
Mortal Education, Joyce Peseroff
How Things Are, James Richardson
Years Later, Gregory Djanikian
On the Waterbed They Sank to Their Own Levels, Sarah Rosenblatt
Blue Jesus, Jim Daniels
Winter Morning Walks: 100 Postcards to Jim Harrison, Ted Kooser

2001
The Deepest Part of the River, Mekeel McBride
The Origin of Green, T. Alan Broughton
Day Moon, Jon Anderson
Glacier Wine, Maura Stanton
Earthly, Michael McFee
Lovers in the Used World, Gillian Conoley
Ten Thousand Good Mornings, James Reiss
The World's Last Night, Margot Schilpp
Mastodon, 80% Complete, Jonathan Johnson
The Sex Lives of the Poor and Obscure, David Schloss
Voyages in English, Dara Wier
Quarters, James Harms

2002
Astronaut, Brian Henry
Among the Musk Ox People, Mary Ruefle
The Finger Bone, Kevin Prufer
Keeping Time, Suzanne Cleary
From the Book of Changes, Stephen Tapscott
What It Wasn't, Laura Kasischke
The Late World, Arthur Smith
Slow Risen Among the Smoke Trees, Elizabeth Kirschner

2003